I0092850

Remember,
I L♡VE YOU

InsideOut Press
PO Box 2666
Country Club Hills, IL 60478

Copyright © 2022 by Cheryl Host

All rights reserved. No part of this book may be reproduced
in any form on by an electronic or mechanical means, including
information storage and retrieval systems, without
permission in writing from the publisher,
except by a reviewer who may quote
brief passages in a review.

First edition October 2022

Illustrations by Theresa Neal
Cover design by Denise Daub
Interior design by Veronica Daub

For more information about publishing services,
please visit www.InsideOutPress.com.

Printed in the United States of America

Library of Congress Control Number:

ISBN: 979-8-9852054-2-8

In honor of Mom and Dad.
&
In memory of Jim.

Remember, I Love You

A Story About Family and Feelings

By Cheryl Host

Hi! My name is Charlie.

I am a very lucky kid.
Let me tell you why.

1 -

I have a big family!

There's Mom and Dad, my big sister, Katie, and my big brother, Mike.

There's Grandma Kate and Grandpa Jim, Nana Dee and Papa Mike.

I love Mom and
Dad very much.

They teach me
about life, love,
and how to be a
good person.

- 4

I think my sister, Katie, and
my brother, Mike, are cool, even though
we sometimes don't
get along.

Katie's friends laugh too much.
Mike's friends play kind of rough.
They call me
"Squirt," not
Charlie.

My pets are amazing!

Happy and I play together, and I take him for long walks.

He kisses me a lot.

I even taught him some tricks, Like "sit" and "speak."

Flipper is fun to watch.
He swims, eats, and sleeps.
This is my second Flipper.
The first one jumped out of the bowl.
He dried out.
I feed Flipper and clean his bowl
when the water gets dirty.

My grandparents are really special!

Grandma and Nana kiss and hug me a lot when we are together. Grandpa and Papa pat me on the head.

We do fun things like read books,
watch movies, go to the park,
eat hamburgers, and swim
in the community pool.

We even baked yummy
cookies for Santa!
We make up
songs that
start or end in
"I love you."

11 -

My grandparents
come to all my
baseball games.

They tell me that
I do a great job
at everything.

They make me smile
and feel so happy.
I know they love me
very much, and I love
them the same way.

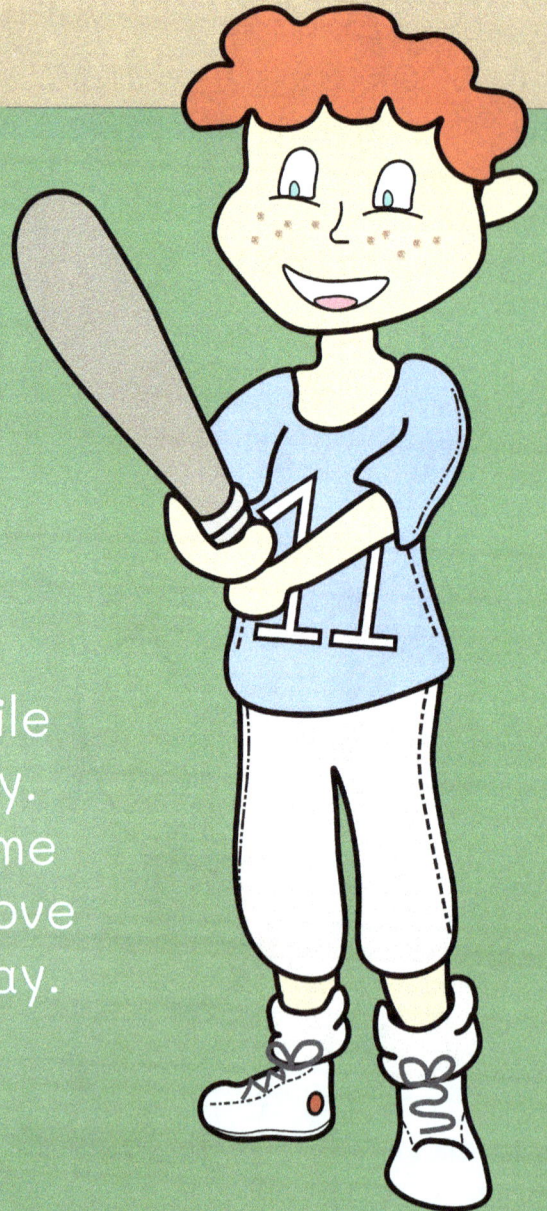

- 12

Grandma Kate
and I have a
secret way of
saying
"I love you."
You touch your
eye,
then your
heart,
and then point
at each other!

13 -

One day, the phone rang, and Mom answered it like she usually does.

When she hung up, she was crying. She was so upset and hugged Dad really tight.

Over and over again, she said, "I can't believe it. Why?" while she cried.

I hugged Mommy, too. I don't like to see her sad.

I asked
Mom to tell
me what
happened.

She told me
that when
Katie and
Mike got
home,
we would
talk
about it
together
as a
family.

I felt worried
and scared.

That night, my parents
explained to us
that Grandma Kate
had died in an accident.

I knew that meant that
I would not be able
to see her anymore.

I would not be able to hug her,
hold her hand, or do
the other stuff we used to do.

I would not be able to smell her flower
perfume when she was near me
or have her kiss mark on my cheek
from her lipstick ever again.

I felt so sad. I cried for a long time.
I felt mad and confused, too.
I fell asleep from crying.

17 -

Later that week, there was a special night at our church when all Grandma's friends and family got together to remember how nice she was.

Some people were really sad and were crying, like me. Some people said prayers.

Everyone hugged Mom and
shook hands with Dad.

My brother, sister, and I behaved
extra well and people hugged us
before they left.

There were lots of flowers
there, even Grandma
Kate's favorite
purple ones.

A few days after all this happened,
Mom and I had a talk
when she was tucking me into bed.
I was still really sad
and confused about
what happened
and I missed
Grandma
Kate a lot.

Mom said
Grandma Kate
    was in heaven now.
It was a beautiful and
        amazing place,
        so I didn't need
        to be so sad.
She reminded me
that we don't always
        understand
why things happen,
    but that's okay.

She also said that
Grandma Kate would
always be with me,
but in a new way now.

I should still think about her
and talk to her about
all the good and bad things
that happen to me.

Mom said Grandma Kate
will be my Guardian Angel!

I love having my own
Guardian Angel!

Sometimes, when I'm
falling asleep,
I think I hear
Grandma Kate's voice.

She whispers to me,
"Always remember,
I love you."

And I say,

"I know, grandma.
I always remember.
I love you."

www.ingramcontent.com/pod-product-compliance
Lightning Source LLC
Chambersburg PA
CBHW052118020426
42335CB00021B/2817